BUNNIES BEHIND BARS
ASTRA PAPACHRISTODOULOU
&
JOHN KILBURN

Newton-le-Willows

Published in the United Kingdom in 2021
by The Knives Forks And Spoons Press,
51 Pipit Avenue,
Newton-le-Willows,
Merseyside,
WA12 9RG.

ISBN 978-1-912211-84-5

Copyright © Astra Papachristodoulou & John Kilburn 2021.

The right of Astra Papachristodoulou & John Kilburn to be identified as the author of this work has been asserted by them in accordance with the Copyrights, Designs and Patents Act of 1988. All rights reserved. No part of this publication may be reproduced, stored in a retrieval system, transmitted in any form or by any means, electronic, photocopying, recording or otherwise, without prior permission of the publisher.

Bunnies Behind Bars

To Gladys.
Wishing you a Happy
Xmas.
Ida x

This book belongs to
John Dunbar Kilburn

Be Safe

This is a tale of distress. This is a tale of sorrow. A tale about four cottontails—tails that belonged to three little bunnies (and one not so little), and their names were: Flopsy, Flimsy, Forrest and Benjamin.

They lived in a long stretch of a bankside by the River Wey, underneath the root of an old English oak tree in Bunshire. Although much of the day was spent inside their warm burrow, resting and cuddling, they were all very active. They hopped on sun-kissed pools of mud at the safest times of the day and often, grazed weeds near a throne made of pebbles just a short distance away from the river.

"Now, my dears," said Mr Benjamin Bye one morning, "you may play to your heart's content, but make sure to stay away from red-eyed humans." The bunnies giggled while splashing and pressing their toes upon the cushions of the stream under the comfort of the blue sky.

Mr Benjamin Bunny, a gentle dad, was very protective of his kittens and insisted with firm but soft voice, "Now run along, and don't get into mischief. We wouldn't want to end up in a laboratory now, would we?"

The Heydays

blue bells, cockle shells,
Flopsy ankle skipping delight
leaves blow, longrope giggling
kittens leisure time in loops

Wild and Soft

nothing feeds the day like
sisterly play and company
there remains no other
season that disperses mist
so gently upon us, and for
that we are grateful

we chase the stretched light
which sometimes leads into
forbidden space - whoever is
caught, the game will go on
in a small chamber furnished
to make a world

Nights That Go By

a long ribbon is cut
by scissors of longing
miles out in the dark
night we stand
undisturbed until we
shift from silk sheets
back to familiar land

A Rebus story: Act out each of the words in the brackets as you are reading the story. Keep it loud.

Before the [SUN] came up on Sunday morning, a rustling sound woke Flopsy up. It sounded like a [BIRD] rustling though [LEAVES]. The little [BUNNY] was worried. She got out of bed and looked out of the [WINDOW], but couldn't find the source of the [SOUND]. Mr. Benjamin, picked up the sleepy [BUNNY] and tucked her back into her [BED]. "Don't worry little one" he said, "you have nothing to be afraid of, as long as [EYE] am here". Flopsy fell back asleep in the comfort of her dad's [FURRY] warmth.

Before the sky opn back into his

Before the came up on Sunday morning, a rustling sound woke Flopsy up. It sounded like rustling through the the little was worried he got out of bed and looked out of the window but find the Mr Benjamin picked him up and tucked him in the sheets dont worry a little bunny

Cornucopia

the sun presides
over our wonder
a lullaby / a growth
a lullaby / a layer
draws us under
aping the rise & fall

portions of rhythm
unmoved rhythms
and unknowing
revolve in enervating
soils of singularity

Connect the numbers below to reveal a happy bunny. Count by 2's.

Menu Du Jour

we sit on a table
by the walled fire
next to a lime tree
and a kind waiter

one father that likes
to spoil his children
he's certainly
not the only one

Human Invasion

inside the walls
of the sandstone cliffs
rising above the Wey
in the midst of silent hunt
humans-in-disguise
with large rusty cages
hang from chalk ceilings

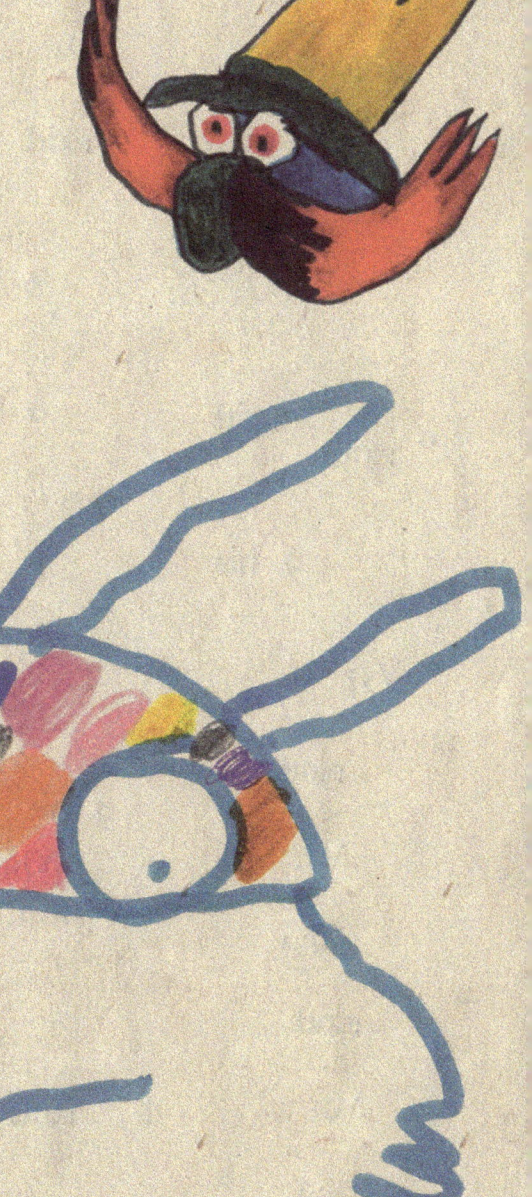

Unexpected

Flimsy hops up
Flimsy hops up
Flimsy hops up
Flimsy hops up
Flimsy hops up
Flimsy hops up
Flimsy hops up
Flimsy hops up
Flimsy hops up
Flimsy hops up
Flimsy hops up
Flimsy hops in

Colour and decorate your box then cut around the edges. Make into a box that can hold Easter eggs and unsuspecting bunnies.

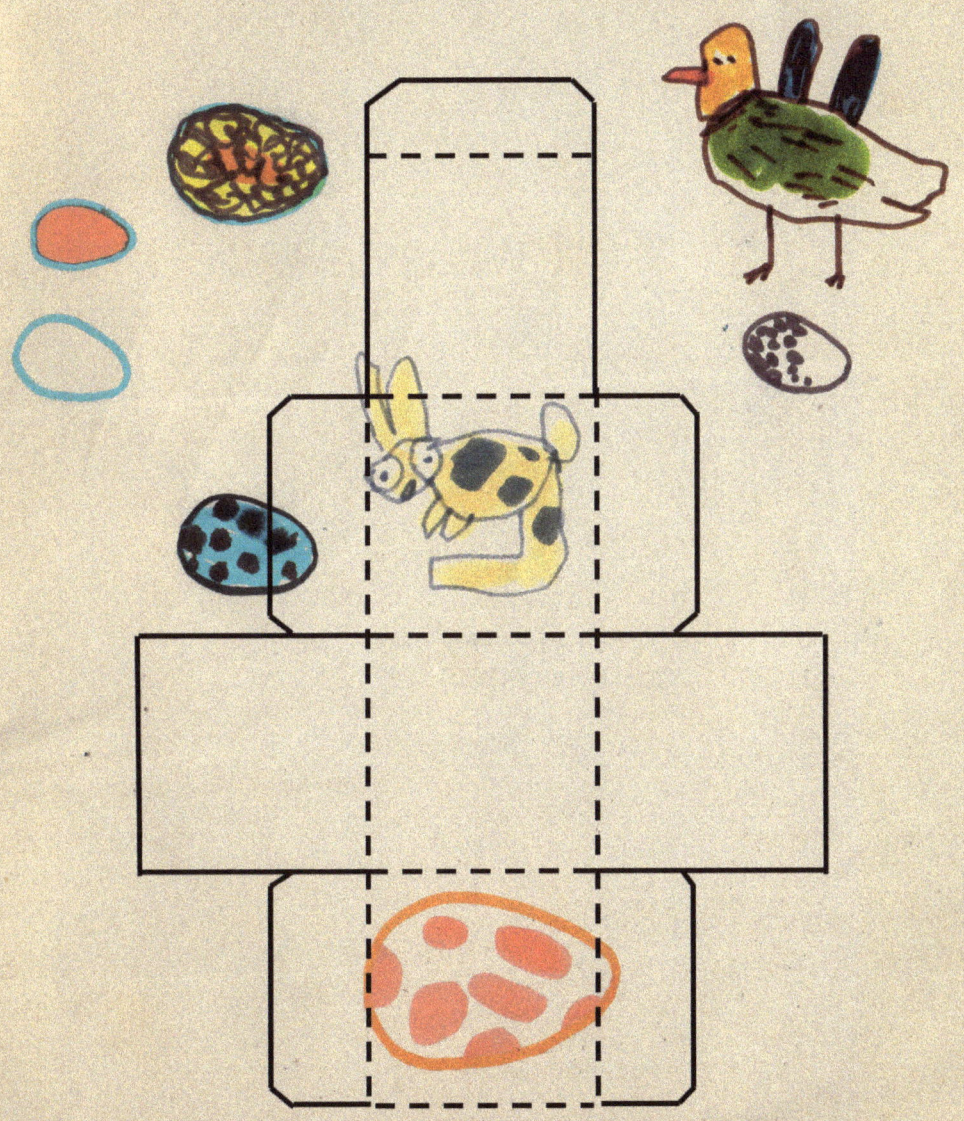

Run Forrest Run

an odyssey across
St. Snowflake's Hill
near the roofless chapel

over green grass
like a runaway train
trying to survive

running in my race
against humans in
contamination suits

during a thunderstorm
shipwrecked, washed-out
& out of breath

All About Human Needs

Have you ever wondered why being scared makes your heart beat faster? The body's reaction to fear is called the "fight or flight" response—bunnies have had it since the beginning of time. Here's how it works: Imagine you're a bunnysaurus living 100,000 years ago, and you come face to face with a hungry saber-toothed human. You have two choices: 1) Run for it (that's flight), or 2) pick up your club and battle the human (that's fight). A final choice (be eaten) doesn't seem like such a good one!

Forrest Cam

REC • 18:05
Flopsy behind bushes.
A human grabs her
by the ears and injects her
a shot of temporal thanatium.
Flopsy loses consciousness.

REC • 18:06
Flimsy screams for help.
The humans show no mercy.
They inject her also, and lock
her away in a rusty cage.

REC • 18:13
Forrest behind hedges
observes the situation quietly.
One of the humans approaches.
Forrest's breathing rate increases.

REC • 18:15
Benjamin is squeaking
in distress to alert his kittens
of the danger. "Kids, hide!"

REC • 18:16
Forrest is grabbed violently
by one of the humans.
She's also thrown into a cage.

REC • 18:18
Benjamin is now out of breath.
Three humans behind him.
"Get the big fluffy one!
Don't let it escape."

REC • 18:21
"Come here, you filthy bastard!"
One of the humans grabs
Benjamin and locks him away.

REC • 18:23
The humans high-five each other
and take a couple of selfies
with the full cages as their prize.

REC • 18:25
Signal breaks.

Catch Me Cause You Can

behind sun-kissed
leafy weeds, he hides
but it's too late

a spring-flood of
memories pass in front
of his eyes like a film

where are they
taking you
Bunny Bye?

from grasslands
and joy into
filthy laboratories

Hidden Grange

a westward trek
across cow fields
leading to a massive
two-storey lab
heavily fortified
with CCTV
and dry brambles
on the entrance
a rusty sign reads

**EMERGENCY
EXIT ONLY**

no unauthorised
persons allowed

overturned sinks
dark and eerie
red-eyed corridors
of chipped paint

PLEASE WASH YOUR YOUR HANDS

no evidence of life
no windows
no attempt to adapt
just control units
to manage this
unethical operation

beyond pitch black
a maze of air ducts
walled with humans
full of resentment

they once had dreams
and ambitions
they now cleanse
themselves
from daily guilt
at the end
of their shift

Payback: An Interval

In 1997 Dr Jay Vacanti
and his team
grew an ear on the back
of a bunny

In 2047 Dr Roger Rabbit
and his team
grew an ass on the face
of a human

Cut out and laminate. Punch two holes ont the sides of your ears and thread elastic through to tie the mask onto your head.

Fear is a Colour

controlled environments
confine the movement
of the captives whose
natural environments
is nothing but controlled

from free & furry to fixed
fur fatales inside a chaos
of fight & force
they give lifeless rooms
frightening colour

Oedipal

forcibly
torn
from
their
screaming
father
and
permanently
separated
from
him

Spinning Flopsy

incessantly spinning in circles **rocking back and forth** pulling out their own fur even biting themselves

tide

LD$_{50}$

LD stands for lethal dose
signifies the single dose of
a chemical needed to kill 50%
killed 50% will kill 50%
pharmaceuticals will
or will not kill 50%
50 kill will 0 defend will

An Internal Monologue

I am mild-tempered and some say
that I am easy to handle
they say that I am the ideal target
because I am small and usually docile
easily restrained, cheap to maintain
they say that I breed prodigiously
and that I am selected mainly due to
practical considerations
how convenient for them!

To whom it may concern,

I write to you out of deep concern for the current state of my health while being unjustly imprisoned by a group of humans for consuming wild conifer needles with my family near the Buntry Woods on October 6th. While I understand why this action upset the local authorities and may have provoked wandering humans, we had not been aware of any warning signs within the area informing natural habitat of such law—we meant no offense by enjoying the outdoors (if this is why you imprisoned us for). This is a speculation as to why this has happened, but I need some formal clarification on the grounds of this unjust capture.

I believe to be a prisoner of conscience, yet I have been detained with no evidence of crime. I strongly urge you to reconsider my imprisonment immediately and release my family and I unconditionally. Until then, I ask you to assure our physical safety while in detention and guarantee that we shall not be subject to any ill treatment. Thanks in advance for your time on this important and urgent matter. I am patiently awaiting your response—please be assured of my most respectful sentiments.

Kind regards,
Professor Benjamin Bye

Professor B. Bye

Hypnodermis

define skin tear.
tissue synonyms.
tissue pronunciation.
tissue translation.

sweet hypnos sweet
for little Flimsy now
blood-soaked tunic
tearing his skin
exposing his bones

wearing masks of
surgical snow fluff
little by little
tearing his skin
exposing his bones

One or More

the led light\\\\\\\\\\grows
//////into my bones////////
sharp & stabbing\\\\\\\\\\\
////////through muscle//////
butter-flow\\\\\\\\\\unable to
move head back////////to the
////////upright position//////
\\precognition\\\white\\light\
///is\\\very///bright\\is///
\\\\\\\\\persistent/////////

**Colour the Easter egg below.
Preferably use blood red.**

Pain Assessment

Case 367
She sits still, very still
in the back of her cage
in a hunched position,
while grinding her teeth
and being oblivious
to her surroundings.

.... E.M

Case 368
He sits still, very still
in the back of his cage
in a hunched position,
while grinding his teeth
and being oblivious
to his surroundings.

.... E.M

Case 369
Decreased fecal production and frantic head elevation. Additionally, she growls and hisses, exhibiting signs of extreme aggression. Put down immediately.

E.M

Find all the words in the grid below – they run in straight lines, in any direction.

T	H	T	C	M	T	T	F	T	M
Y	A	D	K	Y	J	R	Y	K	U
S	E	U	I	Y	U	A	N	A	T
K	M	K	V	W	P	U	K	L	I
R	O	D	R	E	R	M	R	E	L
S	R	A	S	R	S	A	S	R	A
T	R	M	T	B	T	D	N	T	T
L	H	A	S	D	R	L	X	I	E
R	A	G	E	R	A	R	U	N	D
C	G	E	C	C	L	C	Z	J	D
P	E	U	T	S	O	R	R	Y	K
S	O	R	R	O	W	E	G	T	G

sorrow   trauma
sorry   alert
damage   mutilated
haemorrhage   run

A Minute's Silence

marks remembrance
clinical lullaby
will commend shortly
by the albino counter

corrosive chemical
applied onto shaved skin
to determine how much
it takes to kill him

results collated by
Dr Emma Moorfield
experiment over
goodnight Benjamin Bye

Furry Spirit

version of living
HANDLED WITH GLOVES
swarms of living creatures
for me soul is my form
which transcends
the limitations of matter
exterior is a temple
SEALED IN A PLASTIC BAG
they have demolished

Rituals

in their grief they
tear their hair
beyond bouncy curls
& frizz formulas lies
substance & injection
beauty without bunnies
look what you've done

Decide which of the bunnies below is going to survive by drawing a line from each item on the left to its matching item on the right.

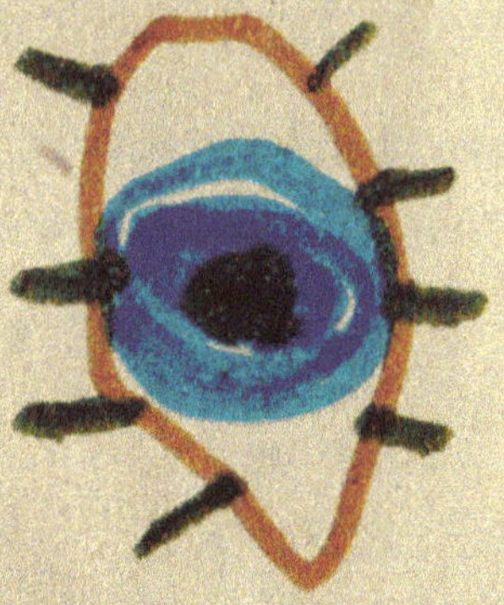

Draize Eye Irritancy Test

a drip into their eyes causes
redness, swelling, discharge
ulceration, haemorrhaging
cloudiness or blindness

a steeping sacrifice for
your Fairy washing up liquid
lipstick and eye liner, your
Mr Right drain cleaner

How many objects are there below?

Supernatural

In a cold dark cell within the animal testing facility—dazed and lifeless, and caked in blood, Forrest looks out from a crevice. Her vision is damaged and her thoughts are scattered. She is clinging to life by thread but she hasn't lost hope. The screams of her neighouring captives pierce her long ears. Her time is short before she must return to the laboratory for more skin testing and other horrors. Suddenly, a breeze of dust enters the cell from the tiny wall crack, and Mr Benjamin's voice hovers above the injured bunny body:

FORREST
Who is this?

GHOST
I am your father's spirit.

FORREST
Daddy, you're back! How did you get here?

GHOST
Now, my Forrest, hear me. There is no time to explain. The morning is near, and so are the evil humans—oh

believe me child, they will be here by dawn. You must find the strength to plan your escape, before it's too late. Employ your sturdy front paws to dig a tunnel leading back to the wild.

FORREST
Which direction do I follow?

GHOST
Head east, towards Carrotville. Dig down to where the minerals are, and then follow the earth seams. Just keep on digging and never look back. Hurry now, my noble child, time's running out! Farewell, farewell, farewell. Remember me.

Tree-Inverted

fever boils between
bare floors and bright
overhead lights
she waited a few hours
for the hum to hush

to have a plan like
trees are springing
to dig and to not stop
to follow the roaring fire
and to never look back

The Great Escape

my first escape was a sweet escape
using my fear as labyrinth
of ever changing tunnel pathways
gravel and sand on top of chalk

inside the air-tight haven
no light, no sound, no humans
only calculated corridors leading to
colliding mud compositions

downwards & brainwards
to escape is to persist, so I kept digging
elongate tubular shapes scraping
the edge of the earth's mantle

Return to Sender

hi mum and Dad
I miss you
Come back
now?
lov you
from FORREST

One-to-one

small talk is just the way
we got it out here—they
sometimes knock on the door
their eyes and whispers
climb to the peak and back

I hide behind a windowpane
with an oil lamp to my guard
I am on the line, how long for?
I meander around thoughts
a light body that doesn't see

the sound of steps and knows
that shadows are minute
passer-byes that eventually
return back to their realities

Will you help this bunny find hope?

Breaking News

Reporter 1: *Welcome back to our breaking news coverage — here at BBB. I am Winston Potters with a horrifying story that's still developing as we speak. We have been informed that the well-known Bunshire professor, Benjamin Bye, is now pronounced dead alongside two of his kits following another illegal experiment at the Houghton Grange last week that was allegedly carried out by a group of humans. Today, I am joined by Scott DeGrass, who will be commenting on this tragedy.*

Reporter 2: *Thank you, Winston. Vile, vile creatures. We are all watching the events unfold in utter shock and fixed to our TVs. Many of our fears have been realised, once more, as the information of new violent attacks by humans continiue to emerge.*

Reporter 1: *Thank you, Scott. Sole survivor and eyewitness, Forrest Bye, confirms that as part of this most recent experiment a dozen fellow rabbits and their kits were taken from Bunshire. The area is now prohibited to animals until things are clearer. We are asking everyone to, please, stay safe and vigilant in their burrows to prevent horrors like this one reoccurring. No animal is safe at the hands of humans. We are, like you, terrified.*

Reporter 2: *Winston, we are looking at an unedited video footage from the scene that clearly shows the violence that took place in the remote laboratory. As of yet, no one has claimed responsibility. Our BBB correspondent Ann DeRabbit is now outside the deadly laboratory, risking her life, to provide us with the latest news on this tragedy.*

Reporter 3: *How devastating the last 24 hours have been for rabbits across the world. Professor Bye's academic contributions to geotechnical engineering have been fundamental to 21st Century tunnel-making. We are now joined by Forrest Bye, the sole survivor of this new tragedy and youngest kit of the late Professor Bye. Forrest is here with us today to report on her traumatizing ordeal. Forrest, what did you experience at the laboratory? We are all ears.*

Reporter 2: *Sorry Ann, we are having trouble hearing Forrest. Can she speak closer to the microphone please?*

Reporter 1: *Right – can someone on the other end bring some tissues? Forrest, I understand that you are experiencing tremendous pain following your family tragedy. Are some days harder than others? What can you tell us about the laboratory conditions? Will you be returning to Bunshire? How has this experience changed you?*

Tears Make Bunnies Uncomfortable

truth is a fixed stone with solid earth
below her feet—she nearly dies
on the road, she wanders grasing land
until the day grows brighter

come in, and have a slice of cake
you will soon forget – they tap your back
you will stand on your own four feet
and enjoy solitude by oaks and crows

the truth is, I wonder on grasing land
the day isn't getting brighter
come in, and have a slice of cake
they keep tapping my back, but don't

know that no day is getting brighter
and I wander the land and mourn alone
in cold days amongst oaks and crows
memory slithers in a snow-heap of grass

#*ByeMemorial*

JUSTICE FOR FLIMSY, FLOPSY AND BENJAMIN

always and forever in our hearts

Confessions of an Orphan

I am

unholy

in my

father's

death .

I lost

my mother

and

my //

father

slew .

Because

I could

do nothing

to

save

them.

We too Flicker

briefly, beneath
moonless nights
the inner oracle
disturbs the slow
mineral silence

Afresh

goodbye childhood, goodbye humans
settling in dry docks of solid earth
back in the roots of the old English oak
I may be abandoned, but I'm not dead

heavy leaves cascade over my muzzle
bunny-in-disguise, without skin,
I am hopping on shallow watersides
this blood-shadowed Bunshire evening

Epilogue

One rainy morning, she took a warm bath at the pebbled Millmead stream. At the end of the day she was so exhausted that she flopped down upon the golden soft sand on the floor of the rabbit-hole, and shut her eyes.

Death caught sight of her again, but Forrest did what she always did when in danger—she kept on running and never looked back. When she arrived at the Bunshire border, an old weeping willow tree used its roots to trip and tie her to the ground. It started strangling her with its long slender branches. It turned out to be another bad dream.

A familiar crippling emptiness stroked her skinless body. It took her years—years of pure and unwavering grieving, to realize that time is the best healer (except for a good night's sleep, of course!). She kept on counting the days in her warm bed until she was ready to explore local nature again. Humans couldn't hurt her anymore.

We warned you that this was a tale of distress. We also warned you that this was a tale of sorrow. A tale that started with four cottontails, and ended with one. A rather brave one.

Acknowledgements

Gratidude to the editors of Berfrois Magazine, Rascal Journal and Stride Magazine for publishing poems from this book, in print and online. Thanks also to L.Kiew for featuring two poems from BBB in her 'Poets in the Library' event at the Westminster Reference Library on June 2019. Lastly, thanks to our editor Alec Newman for bringing this collaborative book to life, and to Aaron Kent, Simon Tyrrell, Helen Nicholas and Steve & Jack Bigglestone-Silk for their kindness and support.

The illustrations for this book have been heavily influenced by the work of Alec Buckels and in particular a worn out copy of Stories of Binnie Buffin (1945) that originally belonged to my Grand Mother. Other notable artistic influences include Looney Tunes and Ken Kagami. J.d.V

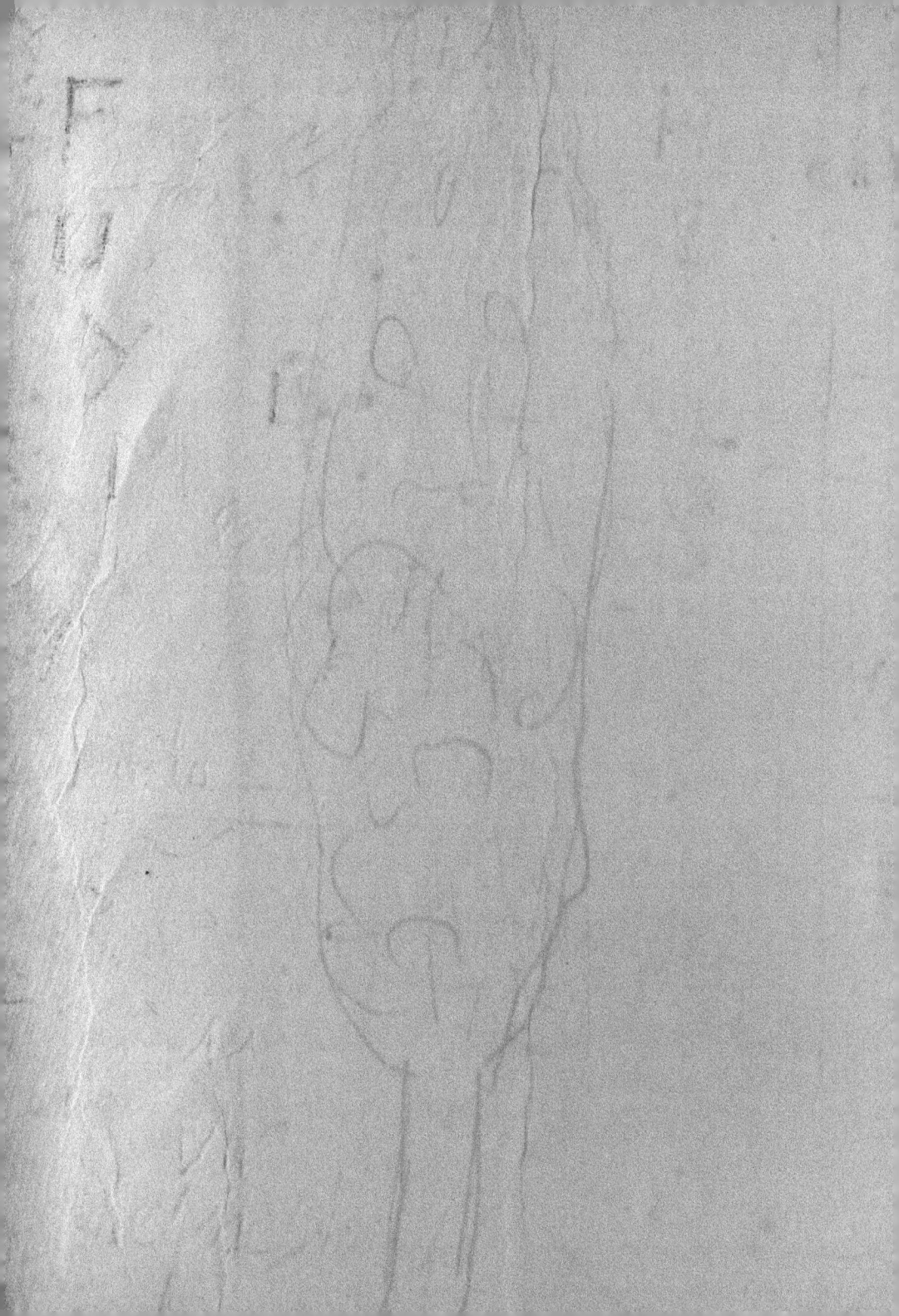

www.ingramcontent.com/pod-product-compliance
Lightning Source LLC
Chambersburg PA
CBHW040258170426
43192CB00020B/2849